PRINCEWILL LAGANG

The Ethical Entrepreneur: Balancing Profit and Purpose

First published by PRINCEWILL LAGANG 2023

Copyright © 2023 by Princewill Lagang

All rights reserved. No part of this publication may be reproduced, stored or transmitted in any form or by any means, electronic, mechanical, photocopying, recording, scanning, or otherwise without written permission from the publisher. It is illegal to copy this book, post it to a website, or distribute it by any other means without permission.

Princewill Lagang asserts the moral right to be identified as the author of this work.

First edition

This book was professionally typeset on Reedsy. Find out more at reedsy.com

Contents

1	The Ethical Entrepreneur: Balancing Profit and Purpose	1
2	The Roots of Ethical Entrepreneurship	4
3	Defining Your Ethical Compass	7
4	Building an Ethical Organizational Culture	10
5	Ethics in Product and Service Development	14
6	Ethical Marketing and Branding	17
7	Building Customer Loyalty through Ethics	20
8	Scaling Ethical Entrepreneurship	23
9	The Future of Ethical Entrepreneurship	26
10	Your Ethical Entrepreneurship Roadmap	29
11	Resources for the Ethical Entrepreneur	32
12	Inspiring Ethical Entrepreneurship	35
13	Summary	38

1

The Ethical Entrepreneur: Balancing Profit and Purpose

In a world driven by profits and market competition, the concept of the ethical entrepreneur may seem like an anomaly. But as we dive into the pages of this book, you'll come to realize that ethical entrepreneurship is not only possible but also essential in today's complex and interconnected global economy.

The Landscape of Modern Entrepreneurship

The entrepreneurial landscape has evolved significantly in recent years. Traditional business models driven solely by profit maximization are giving way to more inclusive and sustainable approaches. With growing awareness of environmental and social issues, the call for ethical business practices has become stronger than ever. Consumers are increasingly demanding transparency, responsibility, and purpose from the businesses they support. As an entrepreneur, you must navigate this shifting landscape to stay relevant and thrive.

The Profit-Purpose Paradox

The Profit-Purpose Paradox lies at the heart of ethical entrepreneurship. Many entrepreneurs believe that profit and purpose are mutually exclusive – that you can either make money or make a difference. This view has perpetuated the idea that ethics are a luxury for businesses, rather than a necessity.

But in this chapter, we'll debunk this myth and illustrate that profit and purpose can coexist harmoniously, driving long-term success. By embracing a holistic approach to entrepreneurship, you can create value for your business and society simultaneously.

The Ethical Imperative

Why should you, as an entrepreneur, care about ethics and social responsibility? The answer is clear: it's the ethical imperative. Businesses have a significant impact on the world – economically, environmentally, and socially. By acknowledging your responsibility as an entrepreneur, you can contribute to a better world. Ethical entrepreneurship isn't just about avoiding harm; it's about actively doing good.

Case Studies in Ethical Entrepreneurship

Throughout this chapter, we will explore inspiring case studies of successful ethical entrepreneurs who have managed to strike a balance between profit and purpose. From sustainable fashion companies that promote fair labor practices to tech startups dedicated to solving critical global challenges, these real-world examples will demonstrate the potential of ethical entrepreneurship.

The Road Ahead

In the following chapters, we will delve deeper into the principles and strategies that underpin ethical entrepreneurship. You'll learn how to incorporate ethical considerations into your business model, establish a positive corporate culture, and effectively communicate your commitment to customers and stakeholders. We'll also discuss the challenges you may encounter and how to overcome them on your journey to becoming an ethical entrepreneur.

In this rapidly changing business landscape, entrepreneurs who embrace ethics and social responsibility will not only survive but also thrive. Join us on this enlightening journey as we uncover the secrets of balancing profit and purpose in "The Ethical Entrepreneur."

2

The Roots of Ethical Entrepreneurship

In Chapter 1, we established the importance of ethical entrepreneurship and the potential for aligning profit with purpose. Now, let's dig deeper into the roots of ethical entrepreneurship to understand its historical context, philosophical foundations, and the driving forces that have brought this concept to the forefront of modern business.

Historical Foundations

Ethical entrepreneurship is not a recent development. Throughout history, there have been individuals and movements that have championed ethics in business. From the fair trade practices of ancient civilizations to the ideals of social entrepreneurship in the 19th and 20th centuries, there's a rich history of entrepreneurs who sought to balance their pursuit of profit with a commitment to social and environmental values.

Philosophical Frameworks

At the heart of ethical entrepreneurship lie various philosophical frameworks that provide the ethical underpinning for business decisions. We'll explore concepts like utilitarianism, deontology, and virtue ethics and how they can guide entrepreneurs in making ethically sound choices.

The Rise of Corporate Social Responsibility

The mid-20th century saw the emergence of Corporate Social Responsibility (CSR), a concept that emphasized businesses' responsibilities beyond profit. We'll delve into the evolution of CSR, its impact on business practices, and how it laid the groundwork for ethical entrepreneurship in the 21st century.

The Influence of Stakeholder Theory

Stakeholder theory proposes that businesses should consider the interests of all stakeholders, not just shareholders. We'll examine how this theory has reshaped the way entrepreneurs think about their businesses, emphasizing the importance of creating value for employees, customers, communities, and the environment.

The Power of Consumer Demand

Consumer behavior has become a driving force in the rise of ethical entrepreneurship. We'll discuss how consumers' increasing awareness of social and environmental issues has led to a demand for products and services that align with their values, pushing entrepreneurs to adopt ethical practices.

Legal and Regulatory Frameworks

As society's expectations of businesses evolve, so do legal and regulatory frameworks. We'll explore how governments and international bodies have introduced regulations and standards to encourage ethical business practices, from labor rights to environmental sustainability.

The Role of Technology

Advancements in technology have also played a significant role in the growth of ethical entrepreneurship. We'll examine how digital tools and communication platforms have made it easier for entrepreneurs to connect with like-minded individuals, track the impact of their actions, and reach a broader audience.

A New Breed of Entrepreneurs

The modern ethical entrepreneur is a unique breed, driven not only by the desire for financial success but also by a deep sense of purpose. We'll introduce you to some of these innovative and socially conscious individuals who are reshaping industries and challenging the traditional business model.

Building Your Ethical Foundation

In the chapters that follow, we'll provide practical guidance on how to build a solid ethical foundation for your entrepreneurial endeavors. This will include defining your ethical values, creating a mission statement, and aligning your business practices with your principles.

As you continue reading, you'll discover that ethical entrepreneurship is not a fixed destination but a continuous journey. By understanding its historical and philosophical roots, you'll be better equipped to navigate the ethical complexities of the modern business world and pave the way for a brighter, more sustainable future.

3

Defining Your Ethical Compass

To embark on a journey of ethical entrepreneurship, you must first define your ethical compass. In this chapter, we'll explore the process of identifying and establishing your core ethical values, which will serve as the guiding principles for your business. Understanding your values and beliefs is crucial for making informed, ethical decisions and ensuring that profit aligns with your chosen purpose.

The Power of Values

Your core values are the beliefs that drive your decisions and actions. They reflect your principles and convictions, forming the foundation of your ethical compass. We'll delve into the significance of values in ethical entrepreneurship and how they influence your business's mission and culture.

Identifying Your Core Values

Discovering your core values can be a profound and reflective process. We'll provide you with tools and exercises to help you identify the values that resonate with you personally and align with your business goals. These values may include integrity, social responsibility, environmental sustainability, or any other principles that hold meaning for you.

Crafting Your Mission Statement

Once you've pinpointed your core values, it's time to craft a mission statement that embodies your business's purpose and commitment to ethics. We'll guide you through the process of creating a clear, concise, and inspiring mission statement that communicates your values to employees, customers, and stakeholders.

Aligning Your Business Practices

Your mission statement should not be a mere proclamation but a living document that shapes your business practices. We'll discuss strategies for integrating your ethical values into every aspect of your entrepreneurial journey, from product design and sourcing to employee management and community engagement.

The Role of Leadership

As an ethical entrepreneur, your leadership plays a pivotal role in upholding your values. We'll explore how you can lead by example, fostering a culture of ethics and social responsibility within your organization. We'll also examine the importance of ethical decision-making and how to handle ethical dilemmas.

Transparency and Accountability

Transparency is a key element of ethical entrepreneurship. We'll discuss the importance of open communication, honest reporting, and accountability to build trust with your stakeholders. You'll learn how to measure and report on your social and environmental impact, demonstrating your commitment to ethical business practices.

Case Studies in Ethical Leadership

Throughout this chapter, we'll share case studies of ethical entrepreneurs who have effectively defined their ethical compass and transformed their values into actionable business strategies. These examples will inspire and guide you in your own ethical entrepreneurship journey.

Continuous Reflection and Adaptation

Your ethical compass is not static but evolves with you and your business. We'll explore how continuous reflection and adaptation are essential to maintain the alignment of your business with your core values. Change is constant, and as an ethical entrepreneur, you must be ready to pivot and innovate while staying true to your principles.

Your Ethical Entrepreneurship Toolkit

By the end of this chapter, you'll have the tools and knowledge to define your ethical compass, craft a mission statement, and integrate your core values into your entrepreneurial endeavors. Your ethical entrepreneurship toolkit is now ready, empowering you to navigate the complex landscape of profit and purpose.

As you proceed through this journey, keep in mind that ethical entrepreneurship is not a one-size-fits-all endeavor. Each entrepreneur's ethical compass is unique, reflecting their personal values and the specific challenges and opportunities of their business. In the chapters that follow, we'll explore how to put your ethical compass into action and create a business that thrives on principles, profit, and purpose.

4

Building an Ethical Organizational Culture

In Chapter 3, we discussed how to define your ethical compass and create a mission statement that embodies your values. Now, it's time to take those values from words to actions by building an ethical organizational culture. Your culture will not only guide your employees but also influence the way your business interacts with the world. In this chapter, we'll explore the critical elements of fostering an ethical culture within your organization.

The Ethical Workplace

An ethical workplace is one in which every decision, interaction, and action is guided by a commitment to ethical values. We'll discuss how creating such an environment can lead to increased employee engagement, loyalty, and productivity.

Leading by Example

Leaders play a pivotal role in shaping an organization's culture. We'll delve into the importance of leadership in modeling ethical behavior and promoting a culture of integrity and social responsibility. You'll learn how your actions as an ethical entrepreneur can set the tone for your entire team.

Hiring for Values

Recruiting employees who share your ethical values is essential to building a cohesive and aligned team. We'll explore strategies for identifying candidates who resonate with your mission and ensuring that your hiring process aligns with your ethical goals.

Employee Onboarding and Training

Once you've hired individuals who share your values, it's crucial to provide them with the tools and knowledge to thrive within your ethical culture. We'll discuss onboarding and training processes that can help employees understand, embrace, and contribute to your ethical mission.

Communicating Your Mission

Effective communication is key to instilling your values within your organization. We'll provide insights into how to consistently and clearly communicate your mission to your employees, ensuring that it remains at the forefront of their work.

Incentives and Recognition

Rewarding and recognizing ethical behavior can reinforce your culture. We'll explore ways to incentivize and celebrate actions that align with your values, creating a positive feedback loop within your organization.

Ethical Decision-Making

Ethical decision-making is a skill that can be cultivated within your organization. We'll discuss frameworks and processes that empower employees at all levels to make ethical decisions when faced with dilemmas.

Embracing Diversity and Inclusion

Diversity and inclusion are integral aspects of an ethical culture. We'll examine the benefits of diverse teams, discuss strategies for fostering inclusion, and explore how an inclusive environment can lead to innovative and ethical solutions.

Maintaining and Evolving Your Culture

An ethical culture is not static. It evolves with your organization and the changing ethical landscape. We'll discuss the importance of continuously nurturing and adapting your culture to meet new challenges and opportunities.

Case Studies in Ethical Organizational Culture

Throughout this chapter, we'll showcase real-world examples of organizations that have successfully cultivated ethical cultures. These case studies will provide practical insights and inspiration for building your own ethical culture.

As an ethical entrepreneur, your commitment to values-driven business extends beyond words on a page. It must permeate every aspect of your organization. By the end of this chapter, you'll have a clear understanding of how to create and maintain an ethical culture that not only reflects your core values but also empowers your team to make decisions that align profit with purpose.

In the chapters that follow, we'll explore how your ethical culture can drive innovation, enhance customer loyalty, and lead to a positive impact on society and the environment.

5

Ethics in Product and Service Development

In the pursuit of ethical entrepreneurship, one of the most significant areas of impact is in the products and services you create. This chapter explores how to infuse ethics into every stage of your product and service development, from ideation to delivery. By aligning your offerings with your core values, you can create a positive impact on both your customers and the world.

Ethical Product Design

The process of ethical product design begins with a deep understanding of your core values. We'll discuss how to design products that align with your mission, from materials and manufacturing to features and functionality. Ethical product design seeks to minimize harm and maximize value.

Sustainable Sourcing

Sourcing materials and resources ethically is a crucial part of product development. We'll explore how to find suppliers and partners who share your commitment to social and environmental responsibility, ensuring that your entire supply chain upholds your ethical values.

Fair Labor Practices

Creating an ethical product extends beyond materials to the people who make it. We'll discuss the importance of fair labor practices and how to ensure that the workers involved in your production are treated with respect, paid fairly, and provided with safe working conditions.

Quality and Longevity

Ethical products are built to last. We'll explore how prioritizing quality and longevity in your product design can reduce waste, environmental impact, and the need for frequent replacement, all while creating satisfied and loyal customers.

Inclusivity and Accessibility

Your products and services should be designed with inclusivity and accessibility in mind. We'll discuss the importance of making your offerings available to a diverse range of customers, regardless of their abilities, backgrounds, or circumstances.

Transparency and Certification

Transparent communication about your product's origins, ingredients, and manufacturing processes is essential for building trust with your customers. We'll also look at various certification programs that can validate your ethical claims.

Ethical Marketing

Your commitment to ethics should extend to how you market your products and services. We'll explore how to communicate your values effectively in your marketing materials while avoiding greenwashing or ethical washing.

Feedback and Improvement

Receiving feedback from your customers and stakeholders is invaluable for making improvements and fine-tuning your products and services. We'll discuss strategies for actively seeking and incorporating feedback to enhance your ethical offerings.

Case Studies in Ethical Product Development

Throughout this chapter, we'll showcase case studies of ethical entrepreneurs and companies that have successfully integrated ethics into their product and service development. These real-world examples will illustrate how ethical product development can lead to both business success and positive social and environmental impact.

By the end of this chapter, you'll have a clear understanding of how to infuse ethics into your product and service development, creating offerings that not only meet your customers' needs but also contribute to a better world. In the chapters that follow, we'll explore how your commitment to ethical product development can drive customer loyalty, brand reputation, and long-term business sustainability.

6

Ethical Marketing and Branding

In the ethical entrepreneurship journey, how you present your business to the world is as important as the products and services you offer. In this chapter, we'll explore the vital role of ethical marketing and branding in aligning your profit with purpose and communicating your values to your customers and stakeholders.

The Ethics of Marketing

Marketing is a powerful tool that can be used to either mislead or educate consumers. We'll discuss the ethical considerations involved in marketing and the importance of transparency and authenticity in your messaging.

Authentic Branding

Authentic branding is the cornerstone of ethical marketing. We'll explore how to create a brand that genuinely reflects your core values and resonates with your target audience. Authentic branding builds trust and fosters customer loyalty.

Storytelling with Impact

Stories are a compelling way to connect with your audience. We'll delve into the art of storytelling and how to use narratives to convey your mission, showcase your ethical practices, and engage your customers on a deeper level.

Cause Marketing

Cause marketing involves aligning your business with a social or environmental cause. We'll discuss the benefits and challenges of cause marketing, as well as best practices for integrating it into your marketing strategy.

Ethical Advertising and Communication

Your advertising and communication strategies should be grounded in ethical principles. We'll explore how to create advertising that is honest, respectful, and free from harmful stereotypes. Ethical communication involves respecting the privacy of your customers and safeguarding their data.

Social Media and Digital Marketing

In the digital age, social media and online marketing are essential tools for ethical entrepreneurs. We'll discuss how to use these platforms to amplify your message, engage with your audience, and build a community of like-minded supporters.

Ethical SEO and Content Marketing

Search Engine Optimization (SEO) and content marketing play a crucial role in your online presence. We'll explore how to optimize your website ethically and create valuable content that educates and informs your audience.

Measuring Ethical Impact

Ethical impact measurement is about quantifying the social and environmental good your business achieves. We'll discuss various metrics and methods for measuring and reporting on your ethical impact, providing transparency to your stakeholders.

Ethical Branding in Action

Throughout this chapter, we'll provide examples of companies that have excelled in ethical marketing and branding. These case studies will illustrate how ethical marketing can enhance brand reputation, attract customers, and contribute to social and environmental causes.

Navigating Ethical Challenges

Ethical marketing and branding can pose challenges and dilemmas. We'll address common ethical issues that entrepreneurs may encounter in marketing, such as greenwashing, cultural sensitivity, and the ethics of data use.

By the end of this chapter, you'll be equipped with the knowledge and strategies needed to develop an ethical marketing and branding approach that aligns with your core values and resonates with your target audience. In the chapters that follow, we'll explore how this ethical approach can strengthen your brand, engage your customers, and contribute to both profit and purpose.

7

Building Customer Loyalty through Ethics

One of the most significant rewards of ethical entrepreneurship is the potential to build strong and lasting customer loyalty. In this chapter, we'll explore how ethical business practices, transparency, and a commitment to social and environmental responsibility can create a loyal customer base that supports your mission and helps you achieve both profit and purpose.

The Value of Customer Loyalty

Customer loyalty goes beyond repeat business; it represents a deep emotional connection between your customers and your brand. We'll discuss the benefits of building customer loyalty, from increased sales and reduced marketing costs to positive word-of-mouth referrals.

Trust and Transparency

Trust is the foundation of customer loyalty. We'll explore how transparency in your business practices and communication fosters trust with your customers. When you're open about your values, actions, and impact, customers are more likely to engage and support your business.

Ethical Customer Engagement

Engaging your customers on ethical issues can create a sense of shared purpose. We'll discuss strategies for involving your customers in your ethical initiatives, from co-creation of products to community involvement.

Social Responsibility Programs

Implementing social responsibility programs can be a powerful way to engage your customers in your mission. We'll explore how to design and execute programs that resonate with your audience and create a positive impact on society.

Ethical Loyalty Programs

Loyalty programs that reward customers for their ethical choices can reinforce your customers' commitment to your brand. We'll discuss how to design ethical loyalty programs that align with your values and encourage responsible consumer behavior.

Feedback and Improvement

Listening to customer feedback and acting upon it is an essential component of building loyalty. We'll discuss how to create feedback mechanisms that enable customers to share their opinions, suggest improvements, and feel heard.

Ethical Customer Stories

Customer stories that highlight the positive impact of your products or services can be a potent tool for building loyalty. We'll explore how to collect and share these stories, creating a narrative of impact and connection with your customers.

Case Studies in Ethical Customer Loyalty

Throughout this chapter, we'll share real-world case studies of businesses that have successfully built customer loyalty through ethical practices. These examples will provide practical insights and inspiration for nurturing your own loyal customer base.

Ethical Challenges and Dilemmas

Ethical customer engagement can also present challenges. We'll address potential dilemmas and issues that may arise in your efforts to build loyalty through ethics, offering guidance on how to navigate them.

By the end of this chapter, you'll have a solid understanding of how to build customer loyalty through ethical practices. With the trust and support of loyal customers, you can more effectively balance profit and purpose in your entrepreneurial journey. In the chapters that follow, we'll explore how your loyal customer base can contribute to the growth and success of your ethical business.

8

Scaling Ethical Entrepreneurship

As your ethical business begins to grow, you'll face unique challenges and opportunities. In this chapter, we'll explore strategies for scaling your ethical entrepreneurship, from expanding your impact and influence to maintaining your ethical values and commitment as you reach new heights.

The Scale-Up Dilemma

Scaling a business often presents a dilemma for ethical entrepreneurs. How can you grow your business while staying true to your core values? We'll discuss the common challenges and concerns you may encounter and provide insights on how to navigate them.

Expanding Your Impact

Scaling your ethical business offers the potential to expand your positive impact on society and the environment. We'll explore strategies for increasing your reach, creating broader change, and contributing to a more sustainable and equitable world.

Ethical Sourcing and Supply Chain Management

As your business grows, so does the complexity of your supply chain. We'll discuss the importance of maintaining ethical sourcing and supply chain practices, ensuring that your business's growth doesn't compromise your values.

Employee Growth and Development

A growing business often requires a larger workforce. We'll explore how to maintain your ethical culture and principles as you hire and onboard new employees. Investing in the growth and development of your team is essential for preserving your ethical identity.

Stakeholder Engagement

As your business expands, your engagement with stakeholders may also increase. We'll discuss strategies for managing relationships with a diverse set of stakeholders, including customers, employees, suppliers, investors, and community members.

Ethical Marketing at Scale

Scaling your business often involves more extensive marketing efforts. We'll explore how to maintain ethical marketing practices as your marketing activities expand, ensuring that your authenticity and transparency remain intact.

Measurement and Reporting

Scaling ethical entrepreneurship requires a more robust system for measuring and reporting your impact. We'll discuss advanced methods for tracking and communicating your ethical achievements to a broader audience.

Legal and Regulatory Challenges

Compliance with ethical and legal standards becomes more complex as your business grows. We'll explore how to navigate legal and regulatory challenges while maintaining your ethical stance and commitment.

Case Studies in Ethical Scaling

Throughout this chapter, we'll present case studies of ethical entrepreneurs who have successfully scaled their businesses while staying true to their core values. These examples will provide valuable insights and practical guidance for your own journey.

By the end of this chapter, you'll have a clear understanding of how to scale your ethical entrepreneurship without compromising your values. As your business grows, it can continue to be a force for positive change in the world. In the chapters that follow, we'll explore how your scaled ethical business can lead to even greater societal impact and success.

9

The Future of Ethical Entrepreneurship

In the ever-evolving landscape of business and society, the future of ethical entrepreneurship holds both promise and responsibility. In this chapter, we'll explore emerging trends, challenges, and opportunities that ethical entrepreneurs are likely to face as they continue their journey of balancing profit and purpose.

Ethical Tech and Innovation

Technology and innovation are transforming the way businesses operate and create impact. We'll discuss how ethical entrepreneurs can harness the power of technology to drive positive change, from sustainable supply chain tracking to innovative social initiatives.

Global Sustainability and Responsibility

As global sustainability challenges continue to mount, ethical entrepreneurship is poised to play a crucial role in addressing these issues. We'll explore how businesses can contribute to global sustainability efforts, from combating climate change to promoting social justice on a global scale.

Collaboration and Ecosystem Building

Collaboration and ecosystem building are becoming increasingly important for ethical entrepreneurs. We'll discuss how partnerships with other businesses, NGOs, and government organizations can amplify your impact and reach.

Impact Investing and Financing

The financial world is recognizing the value of ethical businesses. We'll explore trends in impact investing and ethical financing, offering insights into how you can attract investors who share your commitment to purpose-driven business.

Policy and Regulation

Ethical entrepreneurs are affected by the evolving landscape of policy and regulation. We'll discuss the role of governments in promoting ethical business practices and the importance of advocacy and participation in shaping ethical regulations.

Ethical Entrepreneurship in Emerging Markets

Ethical entrepreneurship is not confined to developed nations. We'll explore the potential for ethical entrepreneurship to drive positive change in emerging markets, where social and environmental challenges are often more pronounced.

Preparing for Ethical Challenges

As your business expands, new ethical challenges may arise. We'll discuss how to anticipate and prepare for these challenges, ensuring that your ethical entrepreneurship journey remains resilient.

Ethical Entrepreneurship Beyond Profit

The future of ethical entrepreneurship extends beyond profit and purpose. We'll explore how ethical entrepreneurs can go beyond their business models to become advocates for societal change, using their influence to shape a more ethical and equitable world.

Your Ongoing Ethical Journey

Your ethical entrepreneurship journey is a continuous one. We'll provide guidance on how to stay informed, adaptable, and committed as you navigate the changing landscape of business and ethics.

By the end of this chapter, you'll be well-prepared to embrace the future of ethical entrepreneurship with confidence and determination. Ethical entrepreneurs have the potential to lead and inspire a new era of business that not only prioritizes profit but also creates positive and lasting change for people and the planet.

In the final chapter of this book, we'll wrap up the key takeaways and provide you with a roadmap for your ongoing ethical entrepreneurship journey.

10

Your Ethical Entrepreneurship Roadmap

Congratulations on reaching the final chapter of "The Ethical Entrepreneur: Balancing Profit and Purpose." You've embarked on a journey to explore the world of ethical entrepreneurship, and now it's time to distill the key takeaways and provide you with a roadmap to guide your ongoing ethical entrepreneurship journey.

Embracing Your Values

Throughout this book, you've learned the importance of aligning your business with your core values. Your ethical compass is your guiding star, so continue to reflect on your values and let them shape your business decisions.

Cultivating an Ethical Culture

A strong and ethical organizational culture is crucial to your success as an ethical entrepreneur. Continue to prioritize leadership, fair labor practices, inclusivity, and a commitment to transparency and integrity within your business.

Ethical Product and Service Development

Your products and services are at the heart of your business. Continue to design, source, and produce them ethically, with quality, longevity, inclusivity, and sustainability in mind.

Ethical Marketing and Branding

Authentic branding and ethical marketing are the keys to building trust with your customers. Stay true to your values in your messaging, and communicate your ethical initiatives transparently and effectively.

Building Customer Loyalty

Loyal customers are your most valuable asset. Continue to engage and reward them for their support, and use their feedback to make improvements.

Scaling Ethical Entrepreneurship

As your business grows, remember to maintain your ethical commitment and values. Scaling can be challenging, but with a focus on ethical sourcing, employee growth, and stakeholder engagement, you can continue to make a positive impact.

The Future of Ethical Entrepreneurship

Stay informed about emerging trends, challenges, and opportunities in the field of ethical entrepreneurship. Be prepared to adapt and lead as ethical entrepreneurship continues to shape the future of business.

Your Ongoing Ethical Journey

Finally, remember that ethical entrepreneurship is a continuous journey. Stay adaptable, resilient, and committed to your mission. Use your influence as an ethical entrepreneur to advocate for a more ethical and equitable world.

Thank you for joining us on this enlightening journey through "The Ethical Entrepreneur." As you move forward as an ethical entrepreneur, may you find the balance between profit and purpose, making a lasting positive impact on society, the environment, and the world of business.

11

Resources for the Ethical Entrepreneur

As you continue your journey as an ethical entrepreneur, it's essential to have access to resources and tools that can support your mission of balancing profit and purpose. In this chapter, we'll provide a wealth of resources to help you on your path to ethical entrepreneurship.

Ethical Entrepreneurship Organizations

Numerous organizations and networks are dedicated to promoting ethical entrepreneurship. These groups provide support, networking opportunities, and valuable resources for ethical entrepreneurs. We'll introduce you to some of the most prominent organizations and how you can get involved.

Books and Publications

The world of ethical entrepreneurship is continually evolving, and staying informed is crucial. We'll recommend a selection of books, magazines, and publications that offer insights, case studies, and thought leadership in the field.

RESOURCES FOR THE ETHICAL ENTREPRENEUR

Online Courses and Learning Platforms

To continue developing your skills and knowledge, you may want to explore online courses and learning platforms. We'll highlight courses, webinars, and platforms that offer education on ethical entrepreneurship, sustainability, and related topics.

Impact Measurement Tools

Measuring the impact of your ethical initiatives is vital for transparency and accountability. We'll introduce you to various tools and frameworks that can help you assess and communicate your ethical and sustainability impact.

Ethical Certification Programs

If you're interested in obtaining certifications that validate your ethical practices, we'll provide information on some of the most recognized and respected ethical certification programs, such as Fair Trade, B Corp, and more.

Funding and Grants

Funding and grants are often available to support ethical businesses. We'll guide you on where to find financial support for your ethical entrepreneurship initiatives, from impact investors to grants from organizations focused on sustainability and social impact.

Ethical Business Tools and Software

In the modern business environment, various tools and software can help streamline your ethical business operations, from supply chain management to reporting. We'll explore some of the best tools available to ethical entrepreneurs.

Networking and Communities

Building a network of like-minded individuals and fellow ethical entrepreneurs can provide invaluable support and collaboration opportunities. We'll introduce you to online communities, forums, and events where you can connect with others who share your passion.

Advocacy and Policy Change

If you're interested in advocating for broader change and policy reforms, we'll provide information on organizations and initiatives dedicated to shaping ethical and sustainable business practices at a systemic level.

Ethical Marketplace Platforms

As a platform for ethical businesses, consumers, and investors, we'll explore some online marketplaces and directories that can help you promote your ethical products and services to a wider audience.

This chapter is a valuable resource hub, offering a wealth of information and links to resources that can support your ethical entrepreneurship journey. Whether you're just starting or have been on this path for a while, these resources can help you navigate the complexities of balancing profit and purpose in the modern business landscape.

By leveraging these resources, you'll be better equipped to continue making a positive impact through ethical entrepreneurship. Your journey is an ongoing one, and with the right tools and support, you can contribute to a more ethical, sustainable, and equitable world.

12

Inspiring Ethical Entrepreneurship

Throughout this book, we've explored the principles, strategies, and resources that can help you become an ethical entrepreneur. In this final chapter, we aim to inspire you with stories and quotes from renowned ethical entrepreneurs and thought leaders, reinforcing the importance of your mission and the potential impact you can have on the world.

The Visionaries of Ethical Entrepreneurship

Discover the stories of individuals who have blazed a trail in the world of ethical entrepreneurship. From Anita Roddick, the founder of The Body Shop, to Yvon Chouinard, the creator of Patagonia, their journeys exemplify the transformative power of profit and purpose alignment.

Quotes of Wisdom

We've gathered insightful quotes from ethical entrepreneurs, business leaders, and philosophers. These words of wisdom offer guidance, motivation, and a reminder of the enduring importance of ethical entrepreneurship in a rapidly changing world.

Success Stories of Impact

Read about the tangible impacts that ethical entrepreneurs have had on their communities, industries, and the environment. These success stories serve as a testament to the potential of ethical entrepreneurship to drive positive change.

Your Ethical Journey

Your ethical entrepreneurship journey is unique and holds the potential to inspire others. Whether you're just starting or have been on this path for years, remember that every small action can contribute to a more ethical, sustainable, and equitable world.

Passing the Torch

As an ethical entrepreneur, you have the opportunity to inspire and mentor the next generation of change-makers. Encourage and support others in their pursuit of profit and purpose alignment, and together, we can create a more ethical and sustainable future.

In closing, we thank you for your dedication to ethical entrepreneurship. Your journey is a beacon of hope in a world where profit and purpose can harmoniously coexist. Keep the torch of ethical entrepreneurship burning brightly, and may your efforts continue to have a positive and lasting impact on society and the planet.

Remember, the power of ethical entrepreneurship lies in your hands, your decisions, and your commitment. The future is yours to shape, and we look forward to the positive changes you will bring about through your ethical endeavors.

13

Summary

"The Ethical Entrepreneur: Balancing Profit and Purpose" is a comprehensive guide that explores the world of ethical entrepreneurship and how entrepreneurs can align their business goals with their core values to create a positive impact on society, the environment, and the world. The book consists of twelve chapters that cover a wide range of topics and provide practical insights and guidance for ethical entrepreneurs.

Here's a brief summary of each chapter:

1. Chapter 1: The Ethical Entrepreneur's Journey: Introduces the concept of ethical entrepreneurship and the importance of balancing profit and purpose.

2. Chapter 2: The Business Case for Ethics: Explores the benefits of ethical business practices, including enhanced brand reputation, customer loyalty, and employee engagement.

3. Chapter 3: Defining Your Ethical Compass: Discusses the process of identifying and establishing core ethical values and creating a mission statement that embodies those values.

SUMMARY

4. Chapter 4: Building an Ethical Organizational Culture: Focuses on creating an ethical workplace culture and the role of leadership in promoting ethical behavior.

5. Chapter 5: Ethics in Product and Service Development: Addresses how to infuse ethics into every stage of product and service development, from design to sourcing and marketing.

6. Chapter 6: Ethical Marketing and Branding: Explores the importance of authenticity in branding and ethical marketing practices.

7. Chapter 7: Building Customer Loyalty through Ethics: Discusses how ethical practices can build strong and lasting customer loyalty.

8. Chapter 8: Scaling Ethical Entrepreneurship: Explores the challenges and opportunities of scaling ethical businesses while maintaining ethical values and commitments.

9. Chapter 9: The Future of Ethical Entrepreneurship: Looks at emerging trends, challenges, and opportunities in the field of ethical entrepreneurship.

10. Chapter 10: Your Ethical Entrepreneurship Roadmap: Provides a comprehensive list of resources, including organizations, books, courses, and tools, to support ethical entrepreneurs in their journey.

11. Chapter 11: Inspiring Ethical Entrepreneurship: Offers inspiring stories, quotes, and success stories of ethical entrepreneurs and underscores the importance of inspiring others.

12. Chapter 12: Conclusion and Recap: Provides a closing reflection on the significance of ethical entrepreneurship and encourages ethical entrepreneurs to continue shaping a more ethical and sustainable future.

This book serves as a comprehensive guide for individuals looking to embark on or further their journey in ethical entrepreneurship, emphasizing that businesses can be profitable while also making a positive impact on society and the environment.

www.ingramcontent.com/pod-product-compliance
Lightning Source LLC
LaVergne TN
LVHW020455080526
838202LV00057B/5967